DevOps For B

A Complete Guide To DevOps Best Practices, Including How You Can Create World-Class Agility, Reliability, And Security In Technology Organizations With DevOps

Craig Berg

Introduction

The term DevOps refers to two primary operations: **development** and **operations**, the two processes that make up the software development process.

We can also consider —and even refer to— DevOps as a culture designed for the promotion of software development and the operations in a collective and collaborative paradigm.

As companies and many businesses adopt cloud-based technologies, DevOps is becoming an increasingly popular approach in the development and maintenance of software. Today, many development teams working on a piece of software often utilize DevOps to build, test, deploy, and maintain the software effectively.

In this tutorial-based book, we are going to cover the complete working of DevOps and the tools used in the processes.

At the end of the book, you should be in a position to perform DevOps using tools such as Ansible, Google Kubernetes, Docker, Git, Jenkins, Nagios, Chef, Puppet, and more.

PS: I'd like your feedback. If you are happy with this book, please leave a review on Amazon.

Please leave a review for this book on Amazon by visiting the page below:

https://amzn.to/2VMR5qr

Your Gift

Let me help you master this and other programming stuff quickly.

Visit

https://bit.ly/codetutorials

To Find Out More

Table of Contents

Section 1: DevOps 101: An Introduction

As mentioned in the introduction, the term DevOps refers to two primary operations: ***Software development*** and ***Operations***, thus the name: DevOps.

DevOps thus encompasses the entire lifecycle of software development. This lifecycle includes operations such as development (programming in general), deployment, testing, and other operations. DevOps helps ensure that the disconnection between the involved parties like software developers, system engineers, and quality assurance engineers is minimal.

DevOps also helps promote collaboration between the Development and Operations departments, from the deployment of the code, to the full production of the end product in an automated and repetitive pattern.

It also helps increase organizational speed, thus delivering applications and services faster. It also allows organizations to compete more strongly in the market and to serve their customers better.

We can also define DevOps as a sequence of development and Information Technology operations governed by collaboration and communication between the involved parties.

The above makes DevOps an essential discipline in enterprises and organizations, especially given its ability to improve quality, speed, and the delivery of the intended application.

DevOps is under the governance of a series of practical methodologies whose aim is to ensure that the developers and the corresponding operations teams work together.

Because of its focus on the delivery of IT services as fast as possible through agile practices in the context of the system-oriented design, it represents a radical change within the IT community.

DevOps integrates the development processes and other operations, thus increasing the software quality and deployment frequency.

Before we proceed further or start discussing the individual pieces of software used in DevOps, we need to understand why we use DevOps over other methods of software production:

Why DevOps?

Some of the primary advantages of using DevOps include:

- Each team involved in the software development process works as a separate unit, which enhances productivity and development efficiency.

- Previously, testing and deployment of pieces of software were two distinct processes performed respectively after the design-build process. That led to time limit constraints after the actual build cycles. Because it combines these processes, DevOps eliminates this 'time wastage.'

- Team Members spend a considerable amount of time on tasks such as designing, testing, and deployment instead of the actual process of building the software.

Since the deployment of the code requires manual input, there is a higher probability of errors during production.

- Teams involved in coding and teams involved in other processes of the software production process do not have synched workflows, thus leading to delays.

The next thing you need to understand is the DevOps architecture features.

DevOps Architecture Features

DevOps architecture offers various key features that include:

Automation

Automation is one of the key features implemented by DevOps. Automation helps reduce the time required in the testing and deployment stages. Automation also helps increase the productivity and the releases of the software. Improved productivity makes detecting and fixing software bugs quickly.

For continuous delivery, each code defined through an automated test builds on other cloud-based services. One example of these services is CloudCI.

Collaboration

DevOps helps create collaboration between the Development and Operations teams. It thus improves the cultural model since teams are more productive. The collaboration also helps strengthen ownership and accountability within the involved teams.

Moreover, because the team shares responsibilities, they tend to work closely and in sync, thus reducing the time required for the deployment of the software.

Integration

At times, software applications may require unification with various external components within the setting.

The stage at which the existing software code combines with a new functionality code in readiness for testing is what we call the *integration phase*. The frequency of implementation of the releases and micro functionalities may lead to significant operational difficulties.

To help overcome problems associated with the integration phase, development teams implement contiguous integration and delivery techniques that make the delivery quicker, safer, and more reliable.

Contiguous integration and testing contribute to continuous development and improvement.

Configuration Management

DevOps offers a reliable environment configuration. This environment helps restrict the application and ensure that it interacts with the resources required by its execution environment. The external configuration files are separated from the source code of the software, while the internal configuration files are not created.

Depending on the execution environment in which the software is running, the configuration files can be written during the deployment stage or loaded during the application runtime.

Advantages And Disadvantages Of DevOps

DevOps has positive and negative impacts on a business. These include:

Advantages

- DevOps is a good approach when dealing with fast development and deployment of applications.

- DevOps can help a business respond and adjust quickly to market changes; faster response can improve business growth.

- DevOps help decrease the application delivery time and transportation costs, thus increasing the business profit.

DevOps helps give clarity to the application development and delivery method because it helps eliminate the descriptive process.

- DevOps also helps improve customer satisfaction as well as experience.

- It simplifies collaboration by making sure all the necessary tools are in the cloud where customers can access then when necessary.

- It leads to better team management, engagement, and productivity by utilizing collective responsibility.

Disadvantages

- DevOps experts or professionals are few, and thus, companies and businesses usually snap up the available ones very fast, thus increasing competition for

- The DevOps process can be more expensive compared to other development paradigms.

Managing or adopting new technology into an existing product is difficult within a short period.

- Lack of knowledge can make operations such as continuous integration and deployment extra challenging.

Prerequisite

DevOps can be a challenge, especially when working within new environments. However, to work with most DevOps tools, you need to learn some universally required skills.

These requirements are: **Competent knowledge working with Linux** and at least **one Scripting Language**. If you are comfortable with the above requirements, proceed to the next section to start learning more about how to start using DevOps:

Section 2: DevOps Lifecycle

The delivery of fully functional applications is a result of the workflow between the Development and the Operations. These two concepts play an essential role in the development of applications.

The development stage consists of tasks such as designing, analyzing the essential requirements, development and testing the software components and frameworks. The Operation stage, on the other hand, consists of tasks such as support for the applications software, administrative processes, and services.

DevOps architecture combines these operations as a way to bridge the gap between development, deployment, and operations, thus delivering the application faster and efficiently.

DevOps primary uses are in the development of cloud-hosted applications and large distributed applications. It utilizes the agile development paradigm in its core architecture, thus ensuring contiguous integration and delivery.

When the development and operation teams work separately from each other, the time required to design, test, deploy, as well as maintain the software increase drastically. Thus, DevOps helps development teams work well together, which increases their overall productivity.

The illustration below shows the major components of the DevOps architecture:

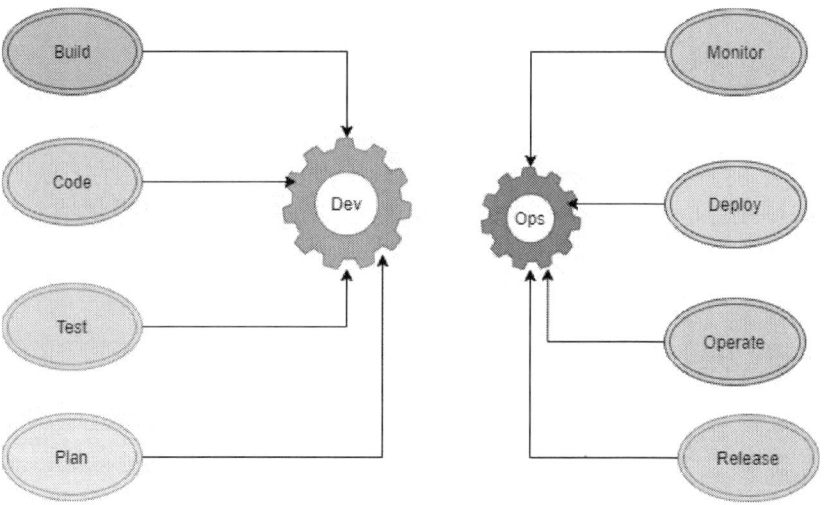

Let's discuss each:

Build

DevOps creates a build-environment that enhances control and maintenance. For example, without DevOps, the cost of resources required per fixed hardware allocation tends to be high. With DevOps, cloud usage allows resource sharing, and thus, establishes codependency between the entire build and set according to the user's needs.

Code

Most good DevOps tools such as git allow users to use code. DevOps also allows users to revert to the previous code in case of unexpected changes. The code is arranged in files and folders and configuration files, thus allowing them to be reused in various projects.

Test

Testing is an essential stage in software development, primarily because it allows developers to test and evaluate how the software works before deployment. Only after successfully passing all the tests is the application ready for production. When using manual testing, a significant amount of time goes into testing and fixing issues that may arise.

DevOps allows for automated testing, thus allowing developers to set up scripts that perform modifications and fix issues faster. That, in turn, helps reduce the time it takes to deploy and produce the application.

Plan

When it comes to planning, DevOps is very efficient. As mentioned, DevOps planning utilizes an agile development methodology. As long as the Development and Operations teams are synched and collaborating, it helps organize the work, which enhances productivity.

Monitor

Constant monitoring helps assess and identify the risk of failure within the application. It helps track the systems and assess the health of the application. DevOps is especially great at monitoring because it creates system log data that is analyzable using third-party applications such as Splunk.

Deploy

Systems can support the automated deployment scheduling mechanism. Having this support enables the cloud platforms and its users to capture accurate insights and optimization factors and trends on their dashboard.

Operate

DevOps is a modern development paradigm that can completely change the traditional approach of development and testing separately. By allowing the teams to operate collaboratively and participate through the service lifecycle, DevOps helps subdivide and modularize tasks.

With DevOps, the operations teams work with the development teams' ideas, and monitoring plans are created, which help meet IT and business requirements.

Release

In DevOps, deployment to an environment is configurable to run automatically, but if the deployment is done during the production environment, it is mainly configured and run manually. That means the numerous processes involved in the release stage are commonly used in the deployment during the production stage, which thus reduces the impact on the involved customers.

Let's discuss the DevOps architecture a bit more deeply:

Section 3: DevOps Architecture

We have mentioned the DevOps architecture and its features. It defines the agile relationship of the deployment and the operations teams from the initial stage of development to the stage of the final product.

In this section, we shall discuss the phases involved in DevOps architecture:

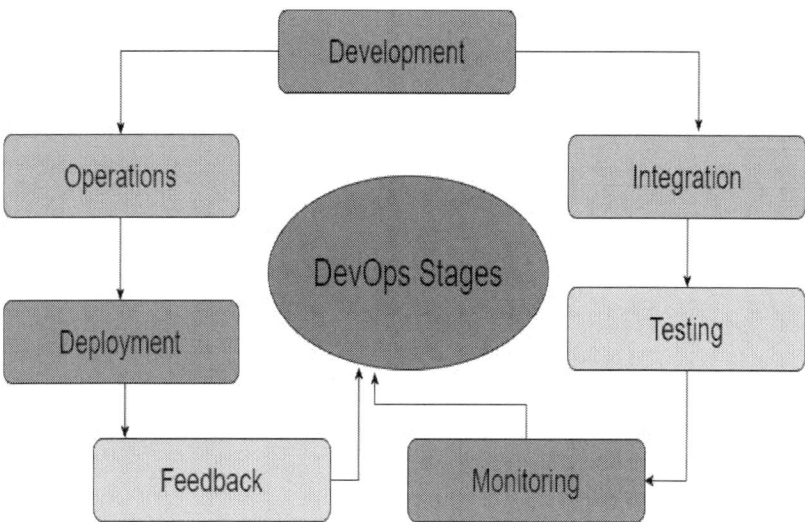

Continuous Development

Continuous development is a very critical stage in the DevOps methodology. It involves the actual planning and the coding for the application.

It's mainly initialized by creating an outline of the application; the developers then create the initial code for the application. At this stage, no DevOps tools are necessary; however, teams are likely to use tools such as IDEs and other code maintaining software.

Continuous Integration

Continuous Integration is a critical stage in the DevOps lifecycle; we can consider it the 'heart' of DevOps.

In this stage, developers have to commit the changes to the already existing code more frequently. This stage also involves the building of the committed changes and allows for early detection and fixing of errors. The code commits can be as frequent as daily or weekly.

When building the source code, teams also carry out other tasks such as unit testing, integration testing, code reviews, and packaging.

The code that has new features and improved functionality without breaking the existing code then becomes part of the current code —by way of integration. This process ensures continuous development and improvement of the software. The integration of the new or updated code must be in a continual manner and work smoothly with systems that reflect changes to the end consumers.

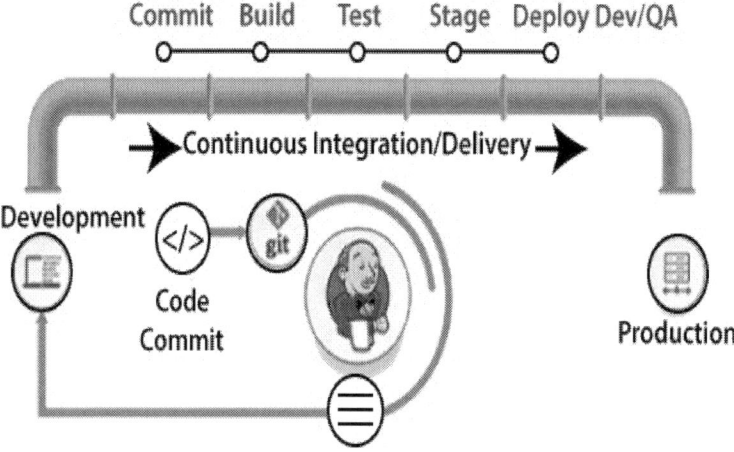

At this stage, several DevOps tools come into play. The tool used most frequently at this stage is Jenkins. If there are any changes in the Git repo, a tool like Jenkins will fetch the code updates and prepare it for the building process. For Jenkins, the build is in the form of an executable .war or .jar file.

After the successful completion of the build process, the code then moves forward to the test server or production servers.

Continuous Testing

We can also refer to this stage as the debugging stage. At this phase, the developed software undergoes testing for bugs.

This stage usually utilizes tools like Selenium, TestNG, JUnit, and others to ensure there's constant and automated testing. Such tools allow for QAs functionality to test multiple code bases in parallel, thus ensuring that there are no functionality flaws. At this stage, the best tool for simulating test environments can be Docker Containers.

Continuous Monitoring

The continuous monitoring stage welcomes the Operations team into the DevOps process. This stage allows the Operations teams to monitor and record all the information about the use of the software. The recorded data then undergoes processing to find out the overall trends and fix problematic areas. The monitoring activity then becomes integrated with the operational capabilities of the application.

The collected data can be in the form of documentation files that produce large scale data concerning the application parameters in a continuous use environment.

Errors that may evolve at this stage, like low memory, server unavailable, high memory usage, also become resolved at this stage. The monitoring phase also handles the security and the availability of the service.

Continuous Feedback

As the name suggests, the feedback phase involves the exchange of feedback between the development and the operations teams. The feedback provided ensures that there is a constant improvement of the software, thus leading to the development of various versions of the same software.

This continuity development methodology is a critical factor in DevOps as it ensures the removal of the unnecessary steps required to update the application from an older version to a new one.

Continuous Deployment

As the name suggests, this stage is the deployment phase of the DevOps Lifecycle. At this stage, the teams deploy the code to the production servers. This stage also ensures that the code works correctly on all the used servers.

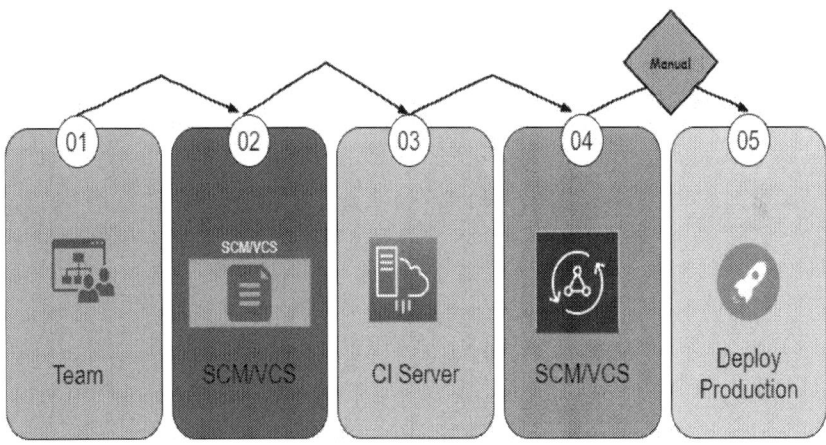

Each newly added code commit is deployed continuously to the deployment servers. At this stage, teams use configuration management tools to help with tasks such as executing tasks frequently and efficiently. Examples of these configuration tools include Chef, Puppet, Ansible, and many others.

This stage also utilizes Containers. The most popular containerization tools include Docker and Vagrant. These tools (and others like them) help enhance consistency across the various stages: development, staging, testing, and production environments, respectively. They are also useful in tasks such as scaling down or up instances in an effective way.

Containerization tools also help maintain consistency between the environments used to develop, test, and deploy the application. Having this consistency ensures that there are no chances of errors or failure once the application is in the production environment. It does this by packaging and replicating the application dependencies and their appropriate packages used in all the stages.

Packaging ensures that the application can run on any computer that meets its requirements. Thus, Containers are an essential tool in the DevOps process.

Continuous Operations

DevOps, and its corresponding operations, depend on the continuity and automation of the releases and code updates that allow the business to accelerate the time required to get to market.

As we have discussed, we can note that continuity is an essential factor in DevOps operations. Continuity removes some of the steps that often cause distraction, time wastage, and errors in the development process.

DevOps thus ensures that the development and production of the software or application occur efficiently to make sure the end product is the go-to, preferred tool for the targeted customers.

Let's discuss DevOps Workflows and Principles.

Section 4: DevOps Workflow and The Principles

The Workflow helps visually describe the overall sequence that provides the input throughout the entire DevOps process. It also describes the actions performed to arrive at the output given in the context of specific processes.

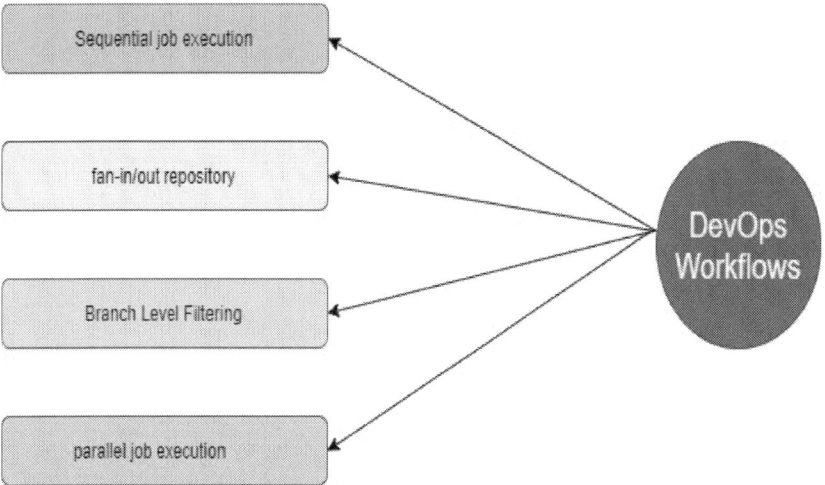

The workflows provided by DevOps provide the ability to separate and organize the top jobs required by the users as well as the ability to replicate or mirror the ideal process in the config jobs.

DevOps Principles

DevOps has three main principles: Automation, Continuous Delivery, and fast reaction to issues and feedbacks within the application environment.

1. **End-To-End Responsibility:** One of the DevOps workflows and responsibility is end-to-end. Here, the DevOps teams have to provide performance support until the applications End-of-Life (EOL) cycle. Having end-to-end responsibility enhances the quality of products.

2. **Continuous Improvement:** DevOps, as we have discussed, focuses on contiguous development and improvement; thus, it minimizes waste and speeds up the growth of the products and the accompanying services.

3. **Automate Everything:** Automation is a key principle in DevOps. It ensures the automation of tasks so that there's as minimal manual work as possible, which is very useful in software development and other areas of business too.

4. **Customer-Centric Action:** Teams working under DevOps must be customer-centric because the end-user will invest in the services and products.

5. **Monitor and test everything:** Monitoring and testing is a primary requirement for DevOps teams

6. **Work as one team:** DevOps is very efficient as it assigns every team tasks that are particular to it. The role of developers, designers, and others are already predefined; all they have to do is collaborate.

Enforcement of all the above principles occurs through the use of DevOps practices. These practices may include deployment, automation, delivery, etc.

DevOps Practices

The following are some of the DevOps standard practices.

- Self-service configuration

- Continuous build processes

- Continuous integration processes

- Continuous delivery processes

- Incremental testing

- Automated provisioning

- Automated release management

Now that you have a fairer understanding of DevOps tools and practices, let's move on to the various tools used in the DevOps process:

Section 5: DevOps Tools

DevOps workflow utilizes a lot of tools. In this section, we are going to cover the popular tools used in DevOps.

Puppet

https://puppet.com/

Puppet is one of the most commonly used DevOps tools. Puppet offers features such as delivery and release of the changes quickly and frequently. It allows automated testing, versioning, and continuous delivery. These features, and many others, give Puppet users the ability to manage the entire code infrastructure without expansion in size.

Features of Puppet

- Real-time context-aware reporting.

- Model and manage the entire infrastructure.

- Defined and continually enforce infrastructure.

- It offers desired state conflict detection and remediation.

- Puppet checks and informs on packages running across the entire infrastructure.

- It eliminates manual work for the software delivery process.

- It helps the developer to bring great software fast.

Ansible

https://www.ansible.com/

Ansible is an open-source engine that allows for automated code deployment, intra-service orchestration, cloud provisioning, and that has other essential Information Technology services and tools.

Ansible makes the work of the DevOps teams so easier, allows automation scaling, and also increases their productivity. Ansible is also very easy to use, especially in deployment, because it does not require agents or infrastructure with custom security on the client-side. Ansible does not push modules to the client; instead, it allows for the local execution of modules on the client-side with the output pushed to the Ansible servers.

Features Of Ansible

- Ansible is easy to use

- Ansible is Open-Source

- It reduces the complexity involved in the deployment of software applications

- It automates most tasks, thus removing repetitive processes

- Manages complex deployment applications and speeds up other processes within DevOps

Docker

https://www.docker.com/

Docker is a popular DevOps tool that uses containers as the base of operations. Docker is a high-end tool that allows developers to build, move, and run distributed applications across systems.

As mentioned during our discussions about containers, all the required packages and dependencies are pre-packaged within the system, allowing applications to cart more easily across devices without errors of compatibility. Docker quickens the process of assembling applications. It is also very suitable for container management.

Features of Docker

- Docker makes the configuration of systems faster and less troublesome

- Docker is useful when it comes to increasing productivity

- It offers the ability to save confidential files within the swarm.

- Its isolated containers are very beneficial when it comes to running applications in isolated environments.

- Docker routes all incoming requests for the known ports on the node that are available to the active container. This functionality allows connection even if no tasks are running on the container nodes.

Nagios

https://www.nagios.org/

Nagios is one of the most useful tools in DevOps operations. Its usefulness is especially in functions such as error determination and fixes using tools such as network, infrastructure, log monitors, and server systems.

Features of Nagios

- Nagios provides a complete set of monitoring tools for desktop and server Operating systems.

- It offers a network analyzing capability that helps identify network bottlenecks and optimize the bandwidth.

- Nagios provides complete monitoring of Java Management Extensions.

- It provides monitoring components for services, applications, and network protocols

CHEF

https://www.chef.io/

Those in the DevOps community are well aware of CHEF because the tool helps scale speed and consistency effectively. CHEF is an open-source and cloud-based tool that uses Ruby encoding for developing essential building blocks. Its primary use is in infrastructure automation, where it helps reduce manual and repetitive tasks within a single infrastructure.

Features of CHEF

- CHEF is highly available

- It handles multiple cloud environments with ease

- It uses popular languages such as Ruby to enforce domain-specific languages.

- CHEF doesn't assume the current status of the nodes within the environments. It uses specific mechanisms to get the current state of the nodes.

Jenkins

https://jenkins.io/

Jenkins is a tool used to monitor the execution of repetitive tasks within an environment; it allows continuous integration within DevOps. Jenkins connects to the server used to create the central build. Jenkins helps integrate project changes more efficiently by discovering the issues rapidly.

Features of Jenkins

- Jenkins helps increase the automation scale.

- Jenkins is easy to use and configure

- It provides a web interface

- It supports continuous integration and delivery

- It has a large selection of plugins that enhance the building and testing of code virtually

- It does not require a lot of maintenance

- it has automatic and easy updates and patches

- It has a high concurrency —since it can distribute tasks across devices.

Git

https://git-scm.com/

Git is probably the most popular tool within the development community. Git is an open-source, distributed version control system. Since Git is freely available to everyone, many DevOps team members prefer it to other paid version control systems.

Git handles minor as well as major projects with high speed and efficiency. It also provides collaboration and coordination among developers working on the same projects. Git offers version control features that make it easier to track and collaborate with fellow programmers within a single workspace. Git use is primarily in distributed version-control systems for DevOps tools.

Features of Git

- Git is free for anyone to use and open-source

- It offers distributed development functionalities

- Git is easily scalable

- Git offers features such as pull-request and merging

- It is one of the most secure DevOps tools

- It completes tasks very fast

- It enables fast release cycles.

SALTSTACK

https://www.saltstack.com/

SALTSTACK is a lightweight tool used to show real-time errors, logs, and queries right within the workstation. SALTSTACK is the go-to solution for software-defined data-centers.

Features of SALTSTACK

- SALTSTACK removes manual and error-filled configurations

- It allows developers to find and fix bugs before production

- It traces details of a web request

- It offers flexible image management, thanks to features such as a private registry.

Splunk

https://www.splunk.com/

Splunk is another tool used in DevOps operations. Splunk makes machine data accessible and usable by every authorized user. Splunk delivers intelligence from the environment operations to the DevOps. This delivery helps companies keep their products secure and productive.

Features of Splunk

- It offers high performance and enhanced monitoring and analytics tools

- Splunk delivers data-driven analytics with high accuracy.

- It offers a unified view of various IT services and functionalities

Selenium

https://www.selenium.dev/

Selenium is a free and open-source portable DevOps framework used for testing web frameworks. Selenium provides an easy to use and interactive interface for developing automatic tests.

Features of Selenium

- Selenium is free to use and open-source

- It is a cross-platform framework available in devices such as Android and iOS

- Selenium is easy to use

- It makes it easy to build keyword-based frameworks for Web Drivers

- It is robust in automated suites and tests.

These ten tools are the most commonly used in DevOps. Next, we shall discuss DevOps automation:

Section 6: DevOps Automation

We have already noted that automation is a crucial practice within DevOps and that Automating everything is a fundamental, DevOps principle.

In DevOps, automation begins from code generation of starter code on the programmer's workspace, moves to the deployment of the code, then goes further to the automatic monitoring of the deployed application, and finally into production.

Automated infrastructure configuration, setup, and application deployment is a salient feature of DevOps Practices. DevOps practices identifications are very dependent on automation to ensure that deliveries happen in a few hours across platforms.

Automation in DevOps helps increase the speed, accuracy, consistency, and reliability of the deliveries. Automation also permeates DevOps processes such as deployment, building, and monitoring.

DevOps Automation Tools

In complex DevOps teams maintaining an extensive IT infrastructure, the automation process can have six main category classifications:

1. Infrastructure Automation

2. Configuration Management

3. Deployment Automation

4. Performance Management

5. Automated Log management

6. Automated Monitoring

In each of the categories named above, the following are the tools often used in each:

Infrastructure Automation

Amazon Web Services (AWS)

https://aws.amazon.com/

Amazon Web Services is one of the tools commonly used in Infrastructure automation. Being a cloud service, it does not require the presence of a physical data center. That means it dramatically reduces the hardware as well as maintenance costs.

The servers provided by AWS are also scalable easily and on-demand. AWS is also configurable to provide more resources and servers as the traffic increases or decreases.

Configuration Management

CHEF

https://www.chef.io/

CHEF is usable in the configuration management stage because of its ability to achieve speed, scalability, and consistency within the predefined environment. CHEF adds effortlessness to complex tasks and config management.

It helps DevOps teams avoid making changes across thousands of servers; all the DevOps teams need to do is perform one staged change at a specific server, and CHEF will automatically broadcast and apply the changes to the other systems.

Deployment Automation

Jenkins

https://jenkins.io/

Jenkins is the go-to tool in deployment automation. It helps simplify the continuous integration and testing processes. Jenkins helps make the integration of project changes more efficiently by automatic error and issue detection as per deployed build.

Performance Management

App Dynamic

https://www.appdynamics.com/

App Dynamic offers real-time performance monitoring tools that help DevOps teams debug issues soon after their discovery.

Log Management

Splunk

https://www.splunk.com/

Splunk helps with tasks such as automated log management. It solves tasks such as storing, aggregating, and analyzing the collected logs in a specific area.

Monitoring

Nagios

https://www.nagios.org/

The Nagios tool helps with system monitoring. It automatically notifies developers when the infrastructure or goes down or fails to function optimally. This feature allows developers to find and correct problems fast.

In the next section, we shall discuss DevOps Engineers:

Section 7: DevOps Engineers

We have discussed the process and the tools used in the DevOps community. Worth mentioning is that these tools would be of no use if no people were using them. In this section, we are going to look at the engineers involved in the DevOps cycle.

What Are DevOps Engineers?

The term "DevOps Engineers" refers to the group of IT professionals who work within the IT hierarchy. They include system operators, software developers, system administrators, and other production staff. Each of these categories of staff ensures that the code is clean and that it works as it should.

DevOps engineers comprehend the entire software development cycle and the respective automation tool used in each stage. They also have skills that allow them to collaborate and communicate with development, testing, deployment, and other operation teams.

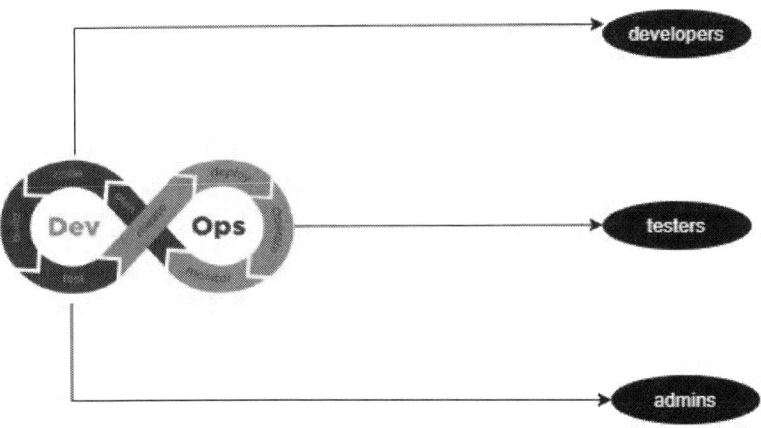

Since DevOps engineers perform coding from scratch, knowledge a software development or programming language is essential. DevOps engineers work with developers by coding and scripting required elements like libraries and configuration files.

In most companies and businesses, a Bachelor's Degree in computer science or a related field is a requirement for a DevOps engineer. Other required skills include knowledge of working with Web technologies such as HTTP and HTTPS, HTML, CSS, ML, Java, AWS, SQL and NoSQL, JavaScript, Linux, and Version Control Tool such as Git.

The Roles And Responsibilities Of A DevOps Engineer

DevOps engineers are full-time workers who usually have various responsibilities that relate to the production and maintenance of the software development cycle.

The following are the primary roles and responsibilities of a DevOps engineer (and the essential skills these engineers need):

- Managing projects efficiently via open standard-based platforms

- Ensuring the timely resolution of system issues using cloud security services

- Developing, analyzing, and evaluating automation scripts on the systems

- Improving quality and reduction of development costs through enhancing productive collaborations

- Improving project visibility via traceability

- Troubleshooting the systems and solving problems across the entire platform or application domain

Because of the essential role they play in the DevOps process, DevOps engineers should be quick learners, have excellent communication skills, be good at solving problems, and have well developed logical thinking capabilities.

Section 8: DevOps Pipelines and Methodologies

In software development, a pipeline is a collection of automated procedures that allow DevOps engineers and developers to dependably and resourcefully compile, build, and deploy code to their production environment platforms.

Components that make up a standard pipeline in DevOps include build automation, test automation, and deployment automation.

A development pipeline utilizes various sets of tools classified into the categories below:

- Build Tools

- Source Control

- Configuration Management tools

- Containerization tools

- Monitoring tools

Continuous Integration Pipeline

A Continuous Integration, mainly called CI, is a development practice where developers check their code against a version-controlled repo to ensure that they are in convention with the set measures and rules.

Automated build DevOps pipelines are mainly activated by the set checks that allow fast and easy error detection and location functionalities.

CI systems offer the following benefits:

- Changes made are easy to integrate into larger codebases.

- There have fewer integration issues, which allows for quick code delivery

- They let other members of the team(s) see what one developer has been working on and where there are issues, to help.

- These systems make it easier to catch and fix bugs earlier, which ensures that coding bugs never get integrated into large codebases. This process helps reduce the debugging process, especially in large code.

Continuous Delivery Pipeline

Continuous delivery or CD refers to the process in which operation engineers and developers deliver bug fixes, patches, features, and configuration changes to the production environments in a quick, reliable, and sustainable process. CD offers code delivery pipelines carried out and executed on demand.

Benefits of Continuous delivery include:

- Provides fast and reliable bug patches and updates

- Allows for continuous delivery that allows teams to work on features and fix bugs in small units known as batches. Working in batches ensures that feedback from the customer is received faster based on the fixed issues and added features.

- It reduces the cost and time of the overall project.

DevOps Methodology

Although not always, DevOps methodology gears more towards cloud options. It accounts for all factors required to ensure a successful approach towards the software development methodology. These factors include people involved, the process applied, and the overall technology used.

Core considerations attached to the use of the DevOps methodology include:

1. **The Teams:** The teams involved in project and cloud management.

2. **Connectivity:** The network access method. These include public, hybrid cloud network, or on-area

3. **Automation:** The automation of the entire infrastructure, including elements like the code, scripting, and deployment resources.

4. **Onboarding Process:** The process involved to get the project running in the cloud.

5. **Project Environment:** The test, development, and deployment environments used.

6. **Shared Services:** Shared and similar services or capabilities that the enterprise offers.

7. **Naming Conventions:** Crucial factors used to track resource utilization and billing.

8. **Defining Standards Role across the Teams:** The permissions granted to access various resources based on the function and responsibility of teams in the DevOps lifecycle.

We shall now discuss one of the best cloud service providers of the modern age

Section 9: Amazon Web Services For DevOps

AWS and DevOps complement each other in the implementation of the entire software development cycle.

In this section, we shall cover the services that make AWS the best cloud provider when working with DevOps.

- AWS CloudFormation

- AWS EC2

- AWS CloudWatch

- AWS Code Pipeline

Let us discuss these services and functionalities briefly.

AWS Cloud Formation

AWS Cloud Formation is a feature that allows developers to release cloud instances and services using frequent and efficient procedures.

AWS offers templates such as AWS EC2, ECS Containers, and S3 storage buckets that allow developers to set up a complete stack without needing to bring together all the required resources.

AWS EC2

AWS EC2 containers give developers and other cloud users the ability to run code containers inside EC2 instance —a fully-functional operating system running on the cloud. This functionality ensures that developers can leverage the features and capabilities provided by the AWS platform.

AWS Cloud Watch

AWS Cloud Watch is a monitoring tool that allows developers to track the resources offered by the AWS. Cloud Watch also makes it easy to utilize other third-party monitoring tools.

AWS Code Pipeline

AWS Code Pipeline, a vital feature within the AWS cloud services, is the management of the Continuous Integration and Development toolset. It offers integration features with popular DevOps tools such as Jenkins, GitHub, and many others.

It also has code Deployment features that give developers the graphical ability to control and manage the flow of the application builds to the production stages.

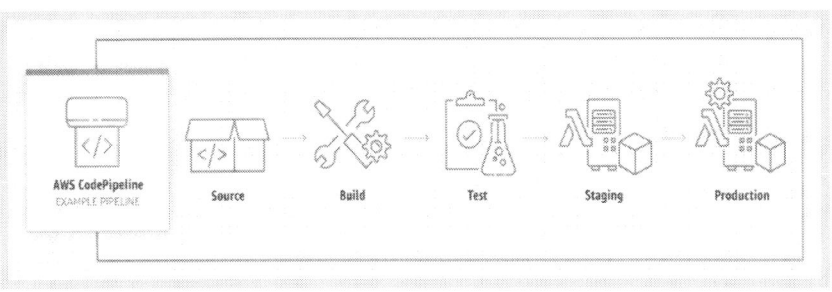

Section 10: DevOps Tools Tutorials

DevOps utilizes numerous tools in its lifecycle. In this section, we are going to cover the most popular tools that will get you set up with DevOps very fast and efficiently. Specifically, we shall discuss how to get started with Git and GitHub.

Git and GitHub Tutorial

This tutorial will give you a complete overview of how to work with Git and its popular Graphical control GitHub.

NOTE: This section looks at beginner and advanced concepts of Git. The ability to work with the command prompt is a prerequisite.

Git is a widely-used, modern version control system. Its primary focus is the management of projects with a high level of efficiency and speed.

As a version control system, Git gives developers the ability to monitor and collaborate in real-time on various projects, which means teams can work on the same projects from the same workspace.

Throughout this section, we will work with Git from the command prompt as well as the Graphical and web interface GitHub. Examples of code used within this tutorial are from a Debian Linux distribution. However, Git is cross-platform and can work on systems such as Windows, Mac, as well as Other Linux distributions.

Introduction

Git is an open-source, distributed version control system whose high functionality allows developers to monitor and track changes within every build with speed and efficiency.

Linus Torvalds developed Git back in 2015 when he was creating the Linux Kernel. Although it's not new, Git is the most popular version control system to date.

Git's development team keeps in mind the fact that minor and major projects will use it, which means it can manage projects worked on by multiple groups of developers with no functionality loss.

Git is mainly the base foundation for various services such as GitHub and GitLab, but can also work as a standalone system. Private and public projects use Git, thus allowing for collaboration from developers around the world.

Apart from being open-source, Git is very easy to learn and offers very high performance compared to other SCM alternatives such as ClearCase, Subversion, Perforce and, CVS.

Features Of Git

Git has some very outstanding features such as:

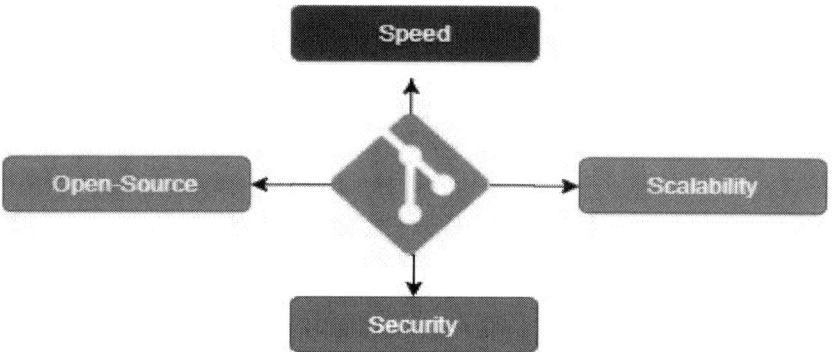

- **Open Source:** Git is an open-source tool that is readily available for anyone to use. It licensing is under the General Public License.

- **Scalable:** Git is highly scalable, which means it can easily handle many users and projects.

- **Distributed:** Distribution is probably one of Git's best features. Its distribution capability allows developers to create clones of an existing repository instead of recreating the entire project to another system. Git also allows each user to have a personal repository that has all the changes made and the commit history of the project. Having this helps reduce the need to have one central system where all changes made have to be sent to every user. Git also allows users to create local repositories, thus removing the need to have every user connecting to the remote repository. Therefore, Developers can perform local build and tests before pushing their changes to the master repository.

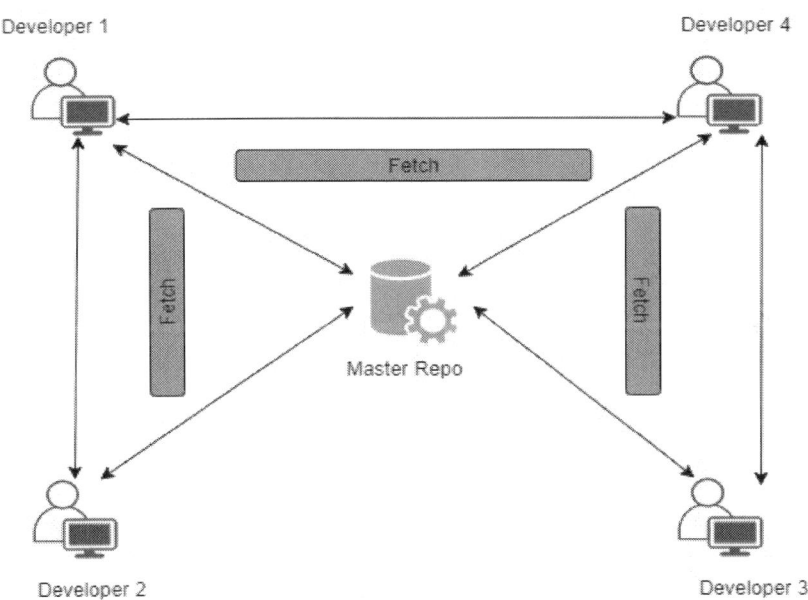

- **Security:** Git is one of the most secure DevOps and version control systems in the world. It utilizes the Secure Hash Functions (SHA1) in its naming and identification of the objects within a specific repository. During checkout, the code commits and files pushed and received to and from the repository are identified by their checksum. Git stores the history in a way that makes sure the Identification of a precise commit is dependent upon the development history that leads up to the current commit. This ensures that after the publication of code, it is near impossible to revert to the previous version.

- **Speed:** We cannot overemphasize just how fast Git is. Git is so fast that it can perform numerous operations and tasks simultaneously. Various numbers of git tasks and processes happen on locally cloned repositories, thus increasing the speed drastically. Even on centralized systems, the communication with a remote server is continuous; therefore, changes and operations reflect quickly. Git speed, which was evaluated by Mozilla, ranked as the fastest version control system compared to other systems. Since Git offers the ability to clone local repos, the fetch speed from local repos is faster compared to fetches on remote servers. Git's base architecture is in the C programming language, which is a relatively fast computing language compared to other high-level programming languages because it ignores runtime overloads. Another cool feature about Git is that it's the brainchild of Linus, which means by design, it works very efficiently with Linux based systems. That makes it capable of handling large repositories that may contain millions and millions of lines of code. As Linus Torvalds said, *"I developed Git with speed and efficiency in mind."*

- **Supports non-linear development:** Git is very good at non-linear development. It supports all-in-one branching and merging of repositories and changes, which in turn helps in navigating the non-linear development. Note that in Git, a single commit represents a branch. Thus, a full branch structure is constructible from the original commit.

- **Branching and Merging:** One of the features that sets apart Git from other SCM tools and services are merging and branching. Git supports the creation and management of various repository branches without conflicts. This functionality allows for the performance of operations such as CRUD (Creation, Reading, Updating, and Deletion) on these branches. The best thing is that branches are not different from master branches and thus do not affect the speed in any way.

NOTE: Branching offers a massive set of features that include:

✓ Creation of separate and independent branches based on new modules of master projects. The branch also has standalone operations such as commits and deletes.

✓ Allows for the creation of different testing and production branches that are merge-able once completed.

✓ It allows for the creation of a separate branch for a new module of the project or commits; this branch is deletable at will.

✓ If required, it is easy to create demo branches and used to test beta versions of products, and where necessary, removed without affecting the master branches.

✓ If developers need to push changes to a remote repo, they do not need to push the changes to all the repositories. All they need to do is push changes to the selected branches or all of them at once.

• **Data Assurance:** Git always ensures the cryptographic integrity of each unit of the entire repository. It performs this by creating unique commit ID to each commit via an SHA algorithm. Having this allows developers to update or retrieve a specific commit based on its unique commit ID. By default, most version control systems do not offer this integrity check.

- **Staging Area:** This unique functionality available in Git is often called a preview of a pending commit. It acts as a central area where developers can format, review, and modify commits before the completion of the push. Having such a central area helps Git collect the changes stored in the staging area and classify them as new commits. Different from full commits, staging commits or staging area commits allow for the addition, removal, and updating of files in it. The staging area is also classifiable as a playfield win that the Git uses to stores changes pending commitment. However, Git does not have a directory that it uses as a staging area for storing objects representing the file changes —also known as blobs. Instead, to perform this task, Git uses files known as "an index."

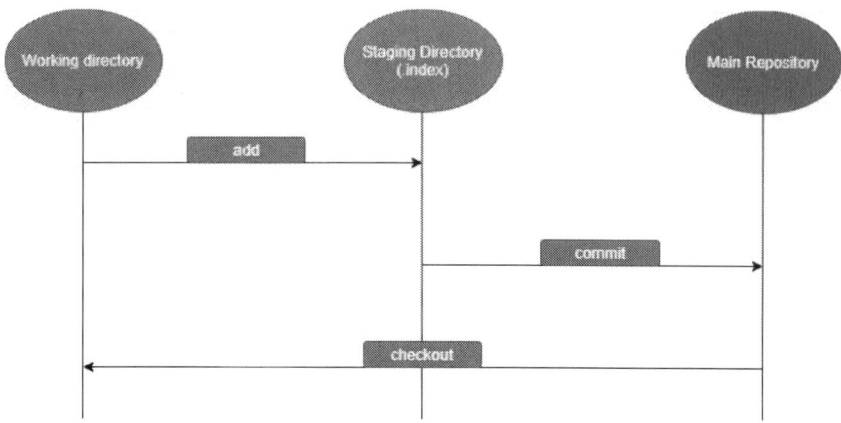

Additional functionality of Git that makes it different from other SCM tools is that it allows developers to rapidly stage various files and then proceed to commit them without having to commit other modified files in the working directory.

- **Maintain the clean history:** One of the most helpful features of Git is the use of services such as Git Rebase. This feature allows developers to fetch the latest commits with the master branch and add code within those files, which ensures there is a clean history of the project.

Benefits Of Git

As a version control tool, Git gives developers and DevOps engineers the ability to keep track of the changes within projects and then push these changed files to the master project base. It enables developers to pull and push changes within a single project and continue to improve, add functionality, as well as fix errors within.

Below are some of the benefits of working with Git:

- **Saves Time**: Git is a super-fast version control tool. It uses simple commands to perform operations that take mere seconds. Being super-fast saves a lot of time, especially compared to using graphical tools and web interfaces such as Gitlab or GitHub.

- **Offline Working:** We cannot exhaustively cover Git's offline working capabilities and features. If working on remote areas where internet connectivity is an issue, Git allows you to perform tasks locally and then push them to the master repository once connected to the internet. Unlike other SCM tools such as SVN in which their capabilities lie within the connectivity to the remotes master or central working repository.

- **Undo Mistakes:** Made a mistake in the code? You can undo this with Git. Git allows developers to undo a code bug or mistake with the files and more. It provides an undo option for almost every function within it.

- **Track the Changes:** Tracking changes within the working repository is a requirement for developers. Git provides such capabilities with commands such as Log, Status, and Diff. It allows developers to real-time-track the status and compared files within working repositories.

Comparison: Git Vs. Other SCM

We have emphasized the benefits and features of Git and displayed why it's the leading version control tool in the entire DevOps community. Why should we choose Git over the other tools?

Let us take a look, shall we?

- **Security and Integrity:** As we have previously mentioned, Git maintains the security and integrity of the content controlled. By using checksums during the transits of the files, Git ensures that no tempering happens on the data and that no information is added or lost along the way. It creates checksums internally from the contents of the files and verifies them when transmitting and storing the data.

- **Popular Version Control System:** Another reason to use Git is its popularity. While that is not the main reason to use it, Git is the number one version control system to hold the maximum number of projects among all SCM systems. Because of its amazing features, speed efficiency, and workflow, it's the go-to tool for most developers.

- **Localization:** The ability to perform all Git Operation on your local machine without needing to connect to a remote repo is a handy functionality. Not requiring internet connectivity whenever you need to work is a significant reason to choose Git over other version control alternatives.

- **Collaboration across Public Open source Projects:** Git hosts most open-source projects, which in this case means GitHub and GitLab. When using Git, it allows developers to collaborate and contribute to open-source projects, thus improving functionalities. It gives developers from all over the world the ability to fix errors and work together to create creative projects. Collaboration also helps junior developers learn from more experienced developers.

- **Getting a Job-added advantage:** Anyone who wants to get a job as a software development engineer should have Git or its related services as part of their resume. Having it is an added advantage.

NOTE: Depending on how you look at it, Git is not a programming language. Using it only requires basic knowledge of how to use the command prompt for the respective Operating systems.

GitHub

GitHub is a repository hosting service for Git. GitHub offers developers features such as access control and collaboration. GitHub primarily uses a web-based GUI interface but offers a desktop GUI version for Windows systems. GitHub hosts the source code and the files for projects and tracks the changes made by developers working on it. GitHub supports all programming languages.

GitHub can offer both distributed version control functionality and source code management SCM, which are core features of Git. It also has collaboration features such as pull requests, bug tracking, task management, role assignment, and more.

Features Of GitHub

GitHub is the most popular collaboration platform in the world. It is a place where developers and teams work together on the same software or application projects to improve it and fix existing errors. It helps programmers collaborate, contribute, and correct errors.

GitHub is a top source for open-source and private projects for multiple programming languages.

The following are some of the primary features of GitHub

- Remote code hosting

- Developers from around the globe can collaborate on the same project

- Graphical interaction and manipulation of repositories and branches

- Git repository hosting

- Supports all programming languages

- Easy assignment, tracking, and management of tasks

- Efficient Project management

- Comment and Conversations among developers

- Offers Integrated Bug and issues tracking

Benefits Of GitHub

GitHub, in general, has two services: *Git* and *Hub*. Together, these services make GitHub, which then offers access to services such as collaboration, task management, team management, and repo hosting.

Some of the most noticeable benefits of GitHub are:

- Makes contributing to Open source projects very easy

- It provides an excellent documentation method for the Repository

- The Changes tracker integrated into GitHub is exceptional

- It allows developers to get help on their projects from other developers around the world.

Git Vs. GitHub

Let us discuss the primary differences between Git and GitHub.

Git is an open-source, freely distributed version control system that allows programmers to collaborate on minor and major projects within the same workspace.

GitHub, on the other hand, is a Git hosting service. It offers a web-based interface with all the functionalities of Git like version control and source code management. It is a standalone software tool with a lot of Git functionalities and more.

To have a clear idea of the primary difference between Git and GitHub, here's a tabular representation of their features.

Git	GitHub
Git is a distributed version control tool that allows programmers to manage their source code changes	GitHub is a cloud-based tool built over Git

Git runs locally on the developer's machine	Git is a cloud service that allows developers to push the locally stored code that is running Git to remote Repositories
Git is (mainly) developed with version control and code sharing as the primary focus.	GitHub focuses more on the centralization of the source code in a remote area .
Git is a command-line tool	GitHub administration is through the web
Git has a Graphical Tool called Git GUI, usable with most operating systems	GitHub has a web-interface as well as a desktop version known as GitHub GUI
Git does not have User management features by default	GitHub offers built-in user management features
Git has Minimalistic tool configuration features	GitHub has an entire market place for tool configuration features

Git Version Control System

We have variously mentioned the term "version control system." Do you know what a version control system is?

A version control tool or system is a software that gives users the ability to track changes to a file or a collection of files within a time window to allow a specific version recall later. Version control systems also give programmers or developers the ability to collaborate from the same workspace.

Version control systems use unique databases that help them track every change or modification done to the code within the existing files. By using these systems, developers are thus able to compare versions of the code from older to newer versions and fix existing mistakes.

Benefits Of Version Control Systems

Version control systems are a critical requirement in the software development process. Developing software without a version control system such as Git is usually unsafe as version control tools provide backups in case of faults or errors on the local machine.

Version control systems also give developers an easy and fast interface that they can use to share their work with others and collaborate. Version control systems also allow developers to maintain a sense of efficiency and agility even as more teams collaborate on the same projects.

Some benefits of using a version control system include:

- Comprehensive change history of files within a repository

- Simultaneous working capabilities

- Branching and merging of repositories

- Trace and revert to previous versions when required.

Types Of Version Control System

We have various types of version control systems. They include:

- Localized version Control System

- Centralized version control systems

- Distributed version control systems

Localized Version Control Systems

The localized version control method is the most common one. Compared to the others, it offers a lot of simplicity; the trade-off, however, is that chances of errors are high.

In a local version control system, developers may forget the directories they are currently working within and accidentally modify the wrong file, which can cause critical errors and even system failure.

A resolve for this issue is the creation of local VCS with simple databases. These databases track all the changes made to the files under a 'revision' control. Local version control systems keep copies of the data.

LOCAL SYSTEM

Centralized Version Control System

CVCS is another type of version control system. Mainly created after the Local version control system, this system cannot allow developers to collaborate with developers on other systems.

Central version control systems have a standalone server that houses versioned files; connected developers check out files from the central, main server.

Compared to Local version control systems, Centralized Version control systems are much more beneficial. Some of their benefits are:

- Each developer on the central system has access to information about the work and what other developers are currently working on in the project

- Centralization allows administrators to have control over other developers lower in the hierarchy

- Centralized version-controlled systems are much easier to work with compared to local systems

- Local systems work in collaboration with central systems that stores and manages the various version of the files within the projects.

Both Local version systems and Centralized version systems have a single point of failure.

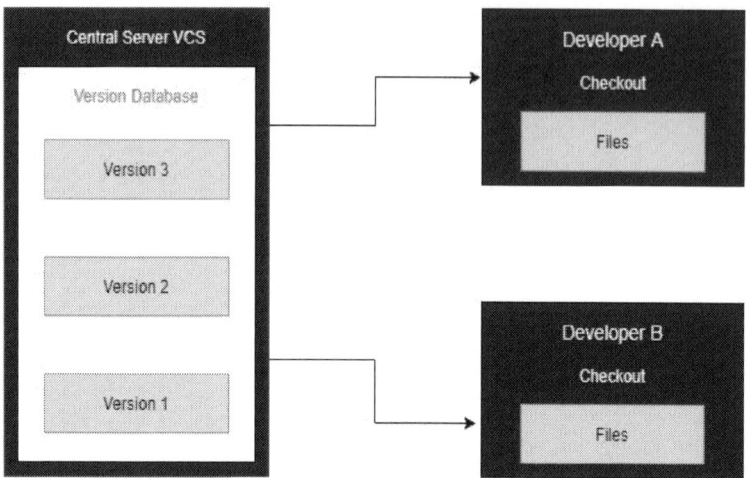

Distributed Version Control System

Centralized version control systems are an improvement over the local version systems.

However, CVCS still has one server that stores all the databases and files. That means such a system has a single point of failure, which is why developers do not prefer it, especially when working with sensitive and crucial projects. A better alternative is the Distributed Version Control system.

In Distributed version control systems such as Git or Mercurial, each user has a local copy of the principal repository. Having this feature ensures that the users do not check out the latest snapshots of the files, but instead, can mirror the entire repo. The cloned or local repository has all the metadata and files within the principal repository.

Distributed Version control systems allow developers to utilize automatic branching and merging of repositories, which speeds up most tasks except pull and push. It also enhances the ability to work without internet connectivity and does not have a single backup location, thus eliminating the single point of weakness in CVCS.

Instead, these systems distribute backups across the workflow. Once a server fails or goes down, other systems collaborating on the project via the server will continue to work. This also helps to restore the server if needed. This means every developer within the cycle has a checkout that behaves like a full backup of the entire repository. Thus, distributed systems do not rely on a central server to store all the metadata and versions of the files within the project.

Centralized Version Control System Vs. Distributed Version Control System

Central version control systems may seem similar to distributed version control systems, but the two have one very significant difference. Centralized version control systems are systems use the client/server architecture, while

Distributed version control systems use the peer-to-peer architecture. In CVCS, the clients connect directly to a central server, while DVCS remain connected throughout.

As you can guess, each system has its advantages and disadvantages. Let us look at the significant differences between these common version control systems.

There are many benefits and drawbacks to using both version control systems. Let's have a look at some significant differences between the Centralized and Distributed version control systems.

Centralized Version Control System	Distributed Version Control System
CVCS uses one central server to store the repositories and delivers information to the connected clients	DVCS provides each client with a local copy of the central repository, and a main server is stored on the servers
It uses the client-server architecture	It is based on the peer-to-peer approach
It is simple and the most straightforward-to-use version of control system.	It is complicated, flexible, and contains features within each repository.
In CVCS, the server provides the latest code to all the clients across the globe.	In DVCS, every user can check out the snapshot of the code, and they can fully mirror the central repository.
Easy to control and	It is relatively fast

contains extra control over users and access by its server	compared to CVCS as you do not require to interact with the central server on each command.
SVN and CVS are the most popular CVCS systems	Popular tools are Git and Mercurial
Easy for beginners to understand and use	May contain complex features that may be challenging for beginners.
In case of failure, data is not accessible across the systems.	In case of server failure, other systems that were collaborating via it do not fail and data can be restored from any client with the required version of the repository

Section 11: Installing Git On Windows, Mac, And Linux

To get started on using Git, you will need to install it. By default, it is pre-installed in most Linux based distributions.

For Windows and Mac systems, you can download it from the official site:

http://www.git-scm.com/downloads.

Once you get the package for your operating system, download and install it. During the installation procedure, you can choose to include Git bash and Git GUI in the context menus.

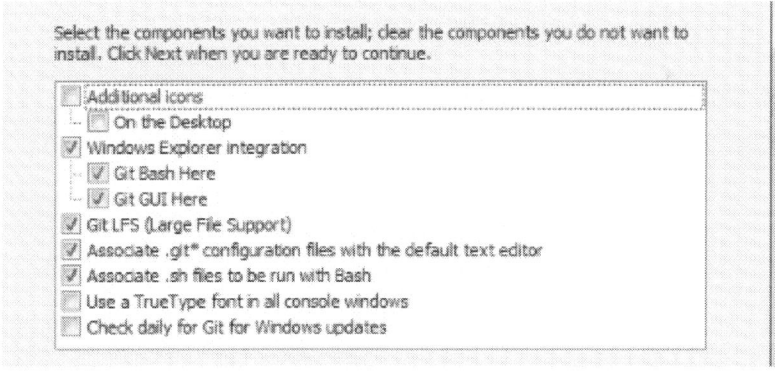

For Linux distributions that do not include it by default, you can install it using your default package manager. For this section, we shall use Debian 10.

1. Ensure that your sources repos are correct.

2. Open the terminal and enter the command

   apt-get update

3. Next, enter the command below to start installing git. Ensure you have root permissions for the installation

   apt-get install git -y

4. Wait until the process is complete and confirm git installation by executing the command

   git –version

5. Once you confirm that Git is installed, you can start to perform Git operations on your system. You may need to configure git first before performing remote operations. Git configuration is available by using the command git config

6. To set your git username, mostly uses GitHub, enter the command git config --global user.name "username"

7. Next, set your email address by using the command git config --global user.email "email@someone.com"

We have many other git environment configurations. Look at the Git documentation to find more information.

Git Commands, Terminologies And Tools

Git Command Line

Git offers numerous ways to interact with it, key of which are command-line, web interface as GUI interfaces. However, if you want the full functionality of Git, the command prompt is the only place to do that.

In this section, we are going to cover the most popular and essential commands to help get you started on Git and its full functionalities.

Basic Git Commands

Here is a list of common and useful commands on daily activities.

a. Git Config

b. git init

c. git clone

d. git add

e. git remote

f. git log

g. git merge

h. git commit

i. git branch

j. git status

k. git pull

l. git push

Let us look at each command in detail.

Git Config

The git config command sets the git user configuration. This is usually an important and first command to execute once installed git. It set user information such as the author and the email address associated with it. The username and email are very crucial and useful during commits on the repositories. The git config also helps set other parameters such as the default text editors.

General General syntax

$ git config --global user.name "Username"

$ git config --global user.email "user@someone.com"

Git Init

The git init command initializes a directory into a git local repository.

General General syntax

$ git init .

The git init . command initialiazes the current directory into a git repository.

Git Clone

The git clone command is used to make a local copy of an existing remote repository via URL. For example, if you want a local copy of GitHub repo, you can copy the URL and clone it using the git clone command.

General syntax

$ git clone URL

Git Add

The git add command adds all the changed files into a staging or indexing area before committing.

General syntax

To add just one file to staging area

$ git add Filename

To add multiple files or all files within the directory.

$ git add *

Git Commit

The Git commit command is useful in two main areas.

Git commit -m

The git command with a -m flag changes the head. It records the file permanently in the version history with a specific message. The -m flag requires a string argument as the message.

General syntax

$ git commit -m " message"

```
SalemaPirate-PC MINGW64 ~/Desktop (master)
$ git commit -m "Hello world"
[master (root-commit) 8583b44] Hello world
 107 fi les changed, 1 insertion(+)
 create mode 100644 Internet Download Manager.lnk
 create mode 160000 Projects/dummy
```

Git commit -a

Any git commit with a -a flag commits any modified files with the repository. It performs git add and commit on the changed files since the last commit.

General syntax

$ git commit -a

Git Status

The git status command displays the current state of the working directory in the staging area. It enables you to see any changes moved to the staging area, those that have changed but are not in staging, and those files not being tracked by Git. The git status command does not, however, give information about previous commits within the project history. This requires the use of the git log command.

General syntax

$ git status

```
Salema@Pirate-PC MINGW64 ~/Desktop (master)
$ git status
On branch master
Changes not staged for commit:
  (use "git add <fi le>..." to update what will be committed)
  (use "git restore <fi le>..." to discard changes in working directory)
  (commit or discard the untracked or modifi ed content in submodules)
        modifi ed:   Projects/dummy (modifi ed content, untracked content)

no changes added to commit (use "git add" and/or "git commit -a")
```

Git Push

Git push is another useful command within the git environment. It uploads a local repo to the remote or master repository. Pushing, in this case, refers to the act of transferring commits from your working local repository to the remote repository. It is the counterpart of git fetch, used to fetch or download remote repo commits into the local repository.

Git branches are configurable using the git remote command. It is good to note that git push overwrites changes. Caution is worth exercising before pushing changes.

git push origin master –

The above command pushes the changes made to the master branch in the remote repository.

General syntax

$ git push master

git push -all

This command pushes all the changes within the entire repository to the remote repository.

General syntax

$ git push --all

Git Pull

The git pull command downloads or receives data from remote git hosting services and merges it to the local working directory.

General syntax

$ git pull URL

```
SalemaPirate-PC MINGW64 ~/Desktop/Projects/dummy (master)
$ git pull
Already up to date.
```

Git Branch

The git branch command lists all the available branches within the repository

General syntax

$ git branch

```
SalemaPirate-PC MINGW64 ~/Desktop/Projects/dummy (master)
$ git branch
* master
```

Git Merge

Git merge command merges a specific branch with a current branch.

General syntax

$ git merge BranchName

```
Salem@Pirate-PC MING#64 ~/Desktop/Projects/dummy (master)
$ git merge master
Already up to date.
```

Git Log

git log checks the entire commit history of a repository.

General syntax

$ git log

If no arguments pass for the git log command, it sorts out the commit history from the most recent one. You can limit the total number of logs displayed by passing a numerical value as the log argument. For example, to display 5 entries, enter the command git log 5

Git Remote

Git remote is the command used to allow you to connect your local repository with your remote repo on a server. Git remote allows you to perform operations such as viewing, creating, and deleting connections to other repositories. The connections act as bookmarks, not direct links to other repositories. It, however, does not provide real-time access to repos.

Git Terminology

Git is an advanced tool that has a load of technical terms and terminologies that can be confusing for beginners. If you want to become a Git master, understanding the terminologies is a crucial step.

In this section, we are going to cover these terminologies, how and when they are used.

Common Terminologies

1. **Branch:** In the git community, a branch is used to refer to a repository that is divergent from the master working repository. Branching is a crucial feature that is available in git and other modern version control tools. A single repository can have multiple branches that also support main git-like operations.

2. **Master:** In git, the term master refers to the default branch in the git repository. If a clone of a repository occurs, the local repository has a single branch called a master branch, which means that a master is a repository default branch.

3. **Checkout:** In git, the term checkout refers to the action of switching different versions of a specific entity. Its use is common when switching between branches in a specific repo.

4. **Cherry-Pick:** This terminology refers to the process of applying a commit from one branch to another. For example, if a developer accidentally commits to the wrong branch, he or she can cherry-pick into another branch without merging the whole branch.

5. **Fetch:** This common term refers to the act of fetching branches, tags from repositories with their corresponding objects in the process of completing the histories. It ensures that the remote-tracking branches remain updated.

6. **Index:** The git index refers to the git staging area that temporarily holds changes between the local working directory and the master repository. It collectively organizes the set of changes that are ready for the commitment process.

7. **Pull:** This is another common term when working with git. The term Pull refers to the act of retrieving data from a remote repository such as from GitHub or GitLab. It

fetches the data and updates the local repository with the changes from the remote repository.

8. **Merge:** Merging refers to the act of putting forked history back. The merge command enables developers to integrate a single branch with data created by git branches.

9. **Git Fork:** A git fork refers to a rough copy of a repository. Once you fork a repository, you can work on it freely; test, build delete, debug, and perform other changes without affecting the original repository. The most common use of forking is when an individual developer wants to test a project and then suggest improvements and fix bugs

10. **Clone:** We have discussed cloning in a previous section. Clone refers to the process on making a local copy of the target repository from a URL.

11. **HEAD:** The term head refers to the representation of the last git commit in the current checkout. In a way, we can refer to it as the current branch. It automatically changes when branches switch using the checkout command, and the head now represents a new branch.

12. **Origin:** Origin refers to the master remote repository where a local repository was cloned initially.

13. **Pull Request:** Pull request is the process through which a developer notifies the team members of a completed feature using their remote server account. Pull requests notify the team to review their code and merge into the master branch if appropriate.

14. **Push:** In git, push refers to the act of uploading the local repository contents to a remote repository.

15. **Rebase:** Rebase refers to the process of combining a collection of commits to a new base of commits. Rebase is a useful function because it makes it possible to change your base branch from one commit to others.

16. **Remote:** In git, the term remote mainly refers to a remote repository hosted on a code hosting server such as GitHub.

17. **Repository:** The term repository or repo is a data structure used by Version Control Systems to store metadata for the files and directories within it. It also has the history of the changes made to the files within. Repositories are usually the base project directories that

contains all the project-related data and files. Each discrete project has discrete repos.

18. **Stashing:** Git stashing is a function that allows developers to switch branches without committing the current working branch. This is very useful when working with incomplete parts of a bigger project.

19. **Upstream and Downstream:** These two terms refere to a repository. The term upstream refers to where a developer clones a repository from the original repository. Downstream refers to any project that integrates your current projects with others. These are not Git terminologies only.

20. **Tag:** Tags mark a commit stage as important. This helps developers to tag a specific commit point for future reference. Their main use is to mark projects point such as versions. There mainly two types of tags.

    a. Light-weighted tag

    b. Annotated tag

21. **Git Ignore:** Git ignore refers to s set of files that are intentionally marked to be untracked by git. Git ignore does not affect files currently tracked by git.

22. **Git Diff:** Git diff refers to a command lint tool that performs diff functions on git data sources. The data source can be branches, commits, files, or working trees.

23. **Git Flow:** GitFlow refers to a branching model developed by Vincent Driessen. GitFlow is a more organized branching model driven by collaboration and scaling. GitFlow has a collection of many git commands; thus, the command accomplished a wide variety of operations.

24. **Git Squash:** In git, the term squash refers to the act of squashing previous commits into a single commit. It group precise changes before sending them. The rebase command also merges various commits into a single commit more powerfully.

25. **Git Rm:** Git rm is a command used to remove files with a working repository. It can remove individual files or a collection. It's main use is remove tracked files from the staging area. It can remove files from working and indexing areas.

Git Tools

For us to explore the full functionality of Git, we use tools. As a standalone tool, Git ha powerful functionalities such as command prompt version and git graphical version called git

GUI. These tools act as interfaces between developers and the git tool.

Git is flexible enough to support other third-party tools, which makes it it even more powerful.

Git Package Tools

Some of the prepackaged tools that come defaulted with git include git bash, git gui, and gitk, which make it possible to edit and commit changes to repositories.

Let us look at each of the prepackaged tools:

GitBash

GitBash is a tool that comes packaged into git for Windows-based environments. It is a graphical tool for Windows that acts as an alternative for the Linux bash tool – only with git as the primary goal.

Git bash provides a Unix bash-like emulation interface for complete git functionality. Those who are not familiar with Unix, Bash, or Bourne Again shell is a terminal interface between the user and the kernel of the operating systems.

The git package installer for windows contains the Bash-Like emulator, utilities for the Windows operating system.

Git Bash Commands

If you poke around, you will note additional commands stored within the /usr/bin directory of the bash emulator. Git bash offers a wide range of functionality on Windows systems. Such functionalities include SSH, SCP, FIND, GREP and more.

Git GUI

The Git GUI is a graphical alternative to the Git BASH tool. The GUI version offers all the functionalities of git bash in an interactive environment in addition to comprehensive visualization tools.

To access the git GUI for Windows, you can right-click and select Git GUI here – if context menu are on or open the command prompt and enter the command git gui.

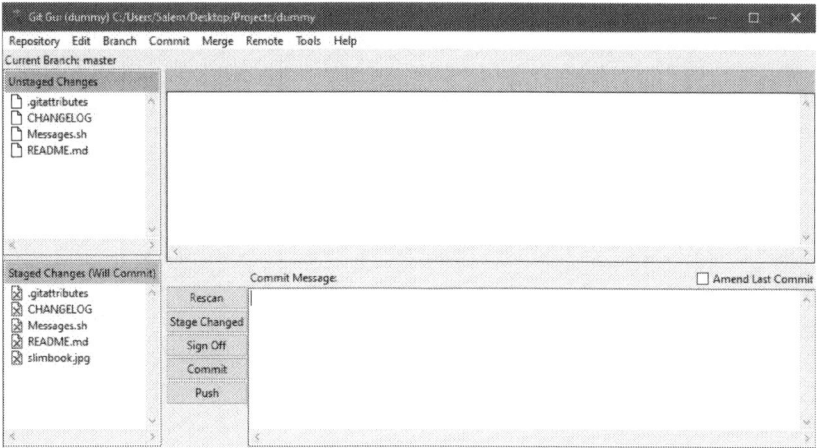

Although git is by itself amazing thanks to its functionalities such as git hui or the history viewing tool gitk, still -party tools and services are continually improving how it works.

Gitk

Gitk is a GUI history viewing tool for git. It is a graphical alternative for git log and git grep with improved and more robust functionalities. It helps developers find changes that were made in the past and help to graphical visualize the project's history.   To launch gitk, navigate to the git repository and enter the command $ gitk [git log options]

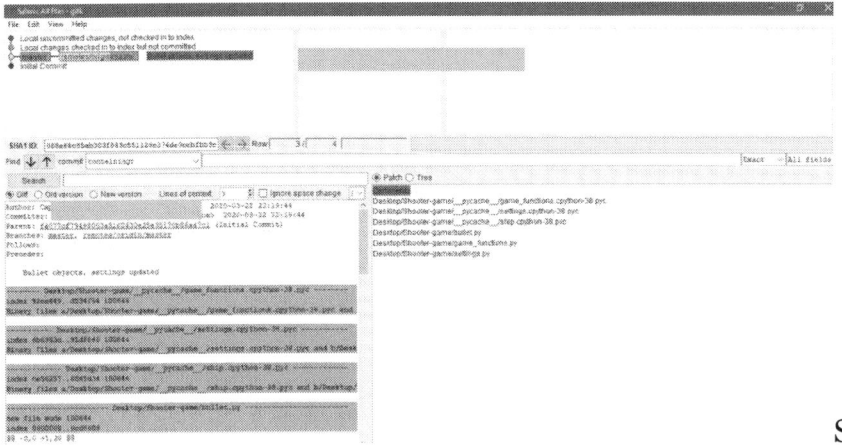

S ince gitk is a GUI version of the git log command, most arguments for git log are usable to modify the output actions.

Git Third-Party Tools

We have various third-party tools that improve the functionality of git by providing simpler and comfortable user interfaces either by web or desktop applications. However, third-party tools are specific to various platforms unless accessed by a web interface.

Some are paid and free. The most popular git Third party tools include:

- GitHub

- SourceTree

- GitKraken

- SnailGit

- GitLab

- Git Extensions

Conclusion

Thank you for reading this guide. I hope that you found it extremely educational and easy to implement.

I'd like your feedback. If you are happy with this book, please leave a review on Amazon.

Please leave a review for this book on Amazon by visiting the page below:

https://amzn.to/2VMR5qr

Printed in Great Britain
by Amazon

BELIEVE

BELIEVE

ACHIEVING THE IMPOSSIBLE

MARK
CAVENDISH

EBURY
SPOTLIGHT

EBURY SPOTLIGHT

UK | USA | Canada | Ireland | Australia
India | New Zealand | South Africa

Ebury Spotlight is part of the Penguin Random House group of companies
whose addresses can be found at global.penguinrandomhouse.com

Penguin Random House UK
One Embassy Gardens, 8 Viaduct Gardens, London SW11 7BW
penguin.co.uk
global.penguinrandomhouse.com

First published by Ebury Spotlight in 2025

1

Typeset by seagulls.net

Printed and bound in Great Britain by Clays Ltd, Elcograf S.p.A.

The authorised representative in the EEA is Penguin Random House Ireland,
Morrison Chambers, 32 Nassau Street, Dublin D02 YH68.

A CIP catalogue record for this book is available from the British Library

Hardback ISBN 9781529149494
Trade paperback ISBN 9781529149500

MIX
Paper | Supporting
responsible forestry
FSC
www.fsc.org   FSC® C018179

Penguin Random House is committed to a sustainable future
for our business, our readers and our planet. This book is
made from Forest Stewardship Council® certified paper.

PROLOGUE